Nora Gallagher

HOW TO STOP A SENTENCE
and other methods of managing words

A Basic Guide to Punctuation

 Addison-Wesley Publishing Company
Reading, Massachusetts • Menlo Park, California
London • Amsterdam • Don Mills, Ontario • Sydney

Library of Congress Cataloging in Publication Data

Gallagher, Nora, 1949-
  How to stop a sentence, and other methods of managing
  words.

  Summary: Uses a humorous touch to explain the use of
  sixteen punctuation marks. Includes illustrative sentences.
  1. English language – Punctuation – Juvenile literature.
  [1. English language – Punctuation] I. Title.
  PE1450.G3   421   81-20628
  ISBN 0-201-10516-0   AACR2
  ISBN 0-201-10517-9   (pbk.)

ABCDEFGHIJ–WZ–85432

First printing: October 1982

Contents

Introduction

When we talk we pause, wave our hands about, and sometimes roll our eyes to let folks know what our words really mean. Without these extra clues, people might misread our thoughts. When we write our ideas, we can't rely on such hints. Everything must be on the paper in black and white for the person to interpret all alone. So in order to give readers some clues, we have punctuation. Besides making things orderly and clear, punctuation often takes the place of our own pauses, hand waving, and eye rolling.

Punctuation comes in many shapes and varieties, and each different piece of punctuation is called a punctuation mark. Some punctuation marks mean "stop." Others are signals for things to come. Many punctuation marks are like ballet directors: they tell you how a sentence should be danced.

For many years there were no punctuation marks. Readers had to learn not only how to read words, but also how to figure out where a sentence began and where it ended. As more and more people learned to read and write, punctuation marks were invented to make the written word easier to understand.

Nobody remembers how to use all punctuation marks all the time. People who write a lot become familiar with certain punctuation marks, especially such common ones as periods, question marks, and commas. They have to look up how to use others, such as brackets, colons, and apostrophes, in a grammar book.

Much of the time punctuation is a matter of common sense. You use the mark that will make the sentence sound closest to the way you speak; you use the mark that *feels* right. But there are certain agreements about how to use punctuation marks correctly. It is helpful to know what those agreements are so that you can use punctuation marks to *dance* beautiful sentences.

Period ●

•

That small, round object up there, disguised as a poppy seed, is actually a *period*.

Periods are needed to stop sentences. Without periods, sentences would crash into each other. Without periods, a reader would have trouble understanding where one sentence ends and another begins. Periods also give you a chance to breathe between sentences.

The most important thing to remember about periods is that they must have a noun and a verb before them. In case you've forgotten, a noun is the name of a person, place, or thing. A verb is an "action" word. It tells you what the noun is or is doing.

This is what would happen if we suddenly ran out of periods:

Once upon a time there was a dragon He lived in a castle in a small town near Chicago, right near the fire department Although the town was small the dragon was very large Often his feet sank through the pavement Sometimes he didn't notice that his tail, which was three blocks behind him, was in Mrs. Little's tulip garden or his rear foot, which was one block behind his head, was in Mr. Small's potato salad If he got excited and swished his tail, the people in the town had to ask the mayor to ask the governor to proclaim it a disaster area

If you read that paragraph out loud, you would soon be out of breath. If you read it to yourself, you'd find that your eyes get tired.

This is how the paragraph would look with periods:

Once upon a time there was a dragon. He lived in a castle in a small town near Chicago, right near the fire department. Although the town was small the dragon was very large. Often his feet sank through the pavement. Sometimes he didn't notice that his tail, which was three blocks behind him, was in Mrs. Little's tulip garden or his rear foot, which was one block behind his head, was in Mr. Small's potato salad. If he got excited and swished his tail, the people in the town had to ask the mayor to ask the governor to proclaim it a disaster area.

Periods are also used to abbreviate words. When you take out the middle or last letters of a word, you put a period at the end of the letters that are left to show people you know there are some missing letters. *Mister* becomes *Mr.,* *February* becomes *Feb.,* and so forth.

That may look like a Captain Hook period, but it is actually a *question mark.*

It is no accident that question marks are shaped like hooks, because asking questions is very much like fishing: you throw out a question and hope for an answer, just as you throw out a hook at the end of a line and hope to catch a fish. It is wise to try to ask the right question: otherwise you are likely to go searching for a great white shark and end up with a goldfish.

What, the mayor wanted to know, is a dragon doing living in this town? Must I arrange a meeting with him? I'd rather take a ride in my new car.

The question mark can make a sentence out of just one word.
Who?
What?
Where?
Why?
When?

Comma ,

,

That is a period that is moving so fast it has a tail behind it. It's called a *comma*.

A comma tells the reader to pause and then go on. It means "something comes after me."

The most common use of a comma is to separate words in a series. This is what would happen if all the commas stopped working:

> **The dragon explained to the mayor that he liked living in a small town because he enjoyed fresh air children quiet streets friendly neighbors the smell of flowers in the air chocolate grasshoppers peanut butter cookies and an occasional glass of lemonade.**

Did the dragon like chocolate and grasshoppers, or chocolate grasshoppers? Did he like peanut butter and cookies, or peanut butter cookies? A small gang of commas would make that sentence sensible:

> **The dragon explained to the mayor that he liked living in a small town because he enjoyed fresh air, children, quiet streets, friendly neighbors, the smell of flowers in the air, chocolate, grasshoppers, peanut butter cookies, and an occasional glass of lemonade.**

Commas are the most frequently used punctuation marks. Writers who don't know how to use them correctly tend to scatter them throughout their sentences as if they were trying to attract comma-eating pigeons. You have to learn to use them carefully or they get out of hand. Here are a few rules to help you.

1) When you are speaking directly to a person or to a group in a sentence, you separate that person or group from the rest of the sentence with commas.

> "Excuse me, Mr. Dragon, but your foot is in the backseat of my car. Don't you realize you are squishing my car?"
> This squashed hunk of metal, my friends, was once the mayor's new car.

2) Phrases in a series are also separated by commas.

> The town where the dragon lived was known for its rainbow-colored rosebushes, backyards full of tree houses, front yards full of grass, a restaurant that sold fried bathtub rings, and a perfectly terrible jail.

3) You use a comma before the words *and, but, for, or,* and *nor* when they connect two main parts of a sentence. You don't use a comma before these words when the second part of the sentence can't stand alone.

> The dragon was sorry about ruining the mayor's new car, but he was not willing to replace it. (*He was not willing to replace it* stands alone.)

> The dragon was sorry about the mayor's new car but was unwilling to replace it. (*Was unwilling to replace it* does not stand alone.)

4) When one part of a sentence introduces another part, you may feel the need for a comma.

If the mayor had been riding a bicycle, the dragon might not have stepped on it.

5) A phrase that adds information about the subject of the sentence is often set off with commas.

The dragon, who had stepped on many cars, always avoided destroying bicycles.

However, a phrase that tells you something so important about the subject that the sentence wouldn't make sense or is inaccurate without it is not set off with commas.

Dragons who step on cars must pay a fine or go to jail.

If you took out *who step on cars* you would get *Dragons must pay a fine or go to jail.* This isn't true.

6) You place a comma after the greeting of a friendly or informal letter, between the date and the year, between a city and state, and after *yes* or *no* when talking to someone.

July 4, 1976

My dear Mr. Dragon,
 Yes, I was so sorry to hear about your mishap.

A friendly neighbor

Semicolon ;

;

This looks like a combination of a comma and a period. It can't decide whether to stop a sentence or to continue to explain its idea. It's called a *semicolon.*

Semicolons are used to join two sentences that are so closely related they should not be separated by a period.

**Old age made the dragon wise; travel made
him witty.**

You could put in an *and* instead of a semicolon *(Old age made the dragon wise, and travel made him witty).* Or you could put a period between the sentence parts and make two complete sentences *(Old age made the dragon wise. Travel made him witty).* That would stop the forward motion, however – like a rock that you run into on your bicycle. A semicolon allows the sentence to flow.

You can't use a semicolon to join two parts of a sentence that can't stand alone (called fragments) or to join one sentence fragment and one real sentence.

**Unfortunately, he could not afford the fine;
and had to go on trial.** *(wrong)*

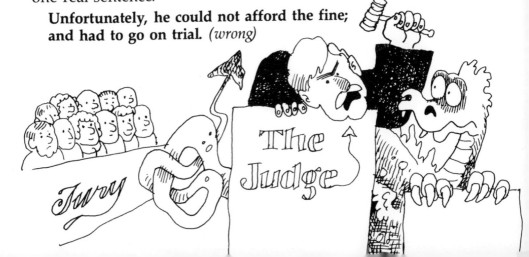

Colon :

:

This is a period on a unicycle. Actually, it's called a *colon*.

A colon looks like two periods in a heap. You'd think it meant "stop, stop!" It doesn't. A colon is like the doorman in front of a hotel. It stops you and then lets you go on. It also opens the door for you.

Colons are most often used before a list. A colon stops readers just long enough to let them know they're in for a long list.

When questioned on the witness stand, the dragon said he liked the following books: The Princess and the Goblins, How to Fry a Human in Ten Easy Lessons, and A Guide to Ballroom Dancing.

Don't use a colon if the list is short.

The dragon also liked Scales from A to Z and Designing Dungeons.

Colons, like semicolons, are also used to join two related sentences, but they are used only when the second part of the sentence explains, expands, or illustrates the first part. (These uses of the colon are less common today. Most people use periods or semicolons instead.)

The dragon said that stepping on the mayor's new car was an accident: he meant to step in a nearby mud puddle. *(explains)*

The dragon recounted his adventurous life to the judge: the first lessons in fire breathing and flying, slaying his first knight, and his first ride on the subway. *(expands)*

The dragon's life had been very exciting: he had slain ten knights and crushed one hundred buses. *(illustrates)*

"Quotation" marks

These are called *quotation marks*. Like twins, they always come in pairs. Quotation marks are used whenever a writer borrows words that belong to someone else. Quotation marks are put around the words characters say in stories. They are used when a reporter reports someone's exact words in a newspaper article. They are also used when a writer uses something someone else has written.

Words borrowed from someone else are called quotations. A quotation mark is placed at the beginning of a quotation and at its end.

The judge's decision was definite. "Mr. Dragon, you must go to jail."

What do you do with other punctuation marks when you are using quotation marks? A comma or period almost always goes inside the second quotation mark.

"Your Honor," the dragon pleaded, "I don't want to go to jail."

If you're wondering whether you put other punctuation marks inside or outside the quotation mark, a good rule to remember is that any punctuation mark at the end of a quotation is *part of the quotation* and goes *before* the quotation mark.

"Please, Your Honor, don't send me to jail!"

A punctuation mark is placed outside the quotation mark only when it is not part of the quotation.

Did the judge say, "Mr. Dragon, you must go to jail"? (The *writer* is asking a question about what the judge said.)

If the writer breaks up a quotation with *he said* or *she screamed* or some other way of describing how someone is speaking, quotation marks are put around each part of the quotation. A comma goes after the first part of the quotation, inside the quotation mark.

"Your Honor," whispered the court clerk, "how will we fit this dragon into our jail?"

Quotation marks are also used when you borrow a word or words from someplace else.

During the trial the mayor referred frequently to his "long lost beloved car."

Quotation marks are used to enclose the titles of poems, songs, television shows, and newspaper or magazine articles. Titles of books, plays, movies, magazines, and newspapers are underlined.

The dragon's favorite song was "Baby, Let Me Light Your Fire."

Although he preferred sonnets, the dragon also enjoyed poems by the local poet Robin Rhyme, such as "Fly Away with Me" and "You Are My Light in the Dungeon of Life."

A play had once been written about the dragon's childhood. It was called <u>First Knight</u> and had never been made into a movie.

If you are quoting someone who is, in turn, quoting someone else, you use *single interior quotation marks,* which are written like this: ' '.

"When I heard the judge say, 'No pinball machines are allowed in jail,' my heart sank," sighed the dragon.

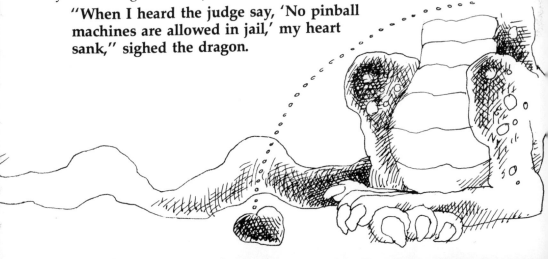

Ellipses ● ● ●

• • •

This punctuation mark looks like a period with two clones following it. They are called *ellipses*. Ellipses always come in threes, like triplets.

Ellipses are used when you leave words out. Most often, ellipses are used in quotations when you want to quote only part of what someone said. You place ellipses wherever there are missing words.

"This jail is dark and dreary," reported the dragon. "It would feel like my dungeon home, except that I have no books to read, no sonnets to soothe me, no friends to talk to, no place to lie down, and my tail is so folded up that I'm not sure it will ever unfold again."

"This jail is dark and dreary," reported the dragon. "It would feel like my dungeon home, except that I have no books to read . . . and my tail is so folded up that I'm not sure it will ever unfold again."

If the ellipses are placed at the end of a quotation, you may put in the proper ending punctuation mark before or after the ellipses, depending on what helps the meaning most. If the punctuation is another period, you should put it first, before the ellipses, right next to the last word.

"This jail is dark and dreary," reported the dragon. "It would feel like my dungeon home, except that I have no books to read. . . ."

Ellipses are also used to show that a thought has trailed off into space.

The judge thought that perhaps he had made a mistake in making the dragon go to jail. Perhaps he should have sent him to Siberia, or asked him to perform a job for the town, or . . .

Occasionally, ellipses are used to show a pause in a sentence or are used for dramatic effect. You should be careful not to use them too often for this purpose, however. You may end up with writing that sounds breathless and silly.

Why, that looks like . . . the dragon!

Do you suppose . . . that could be . . . the dragon? (Ellipses are probably unnecessary here.)

(Parentheses)

( )

These are called *parentheses*. You can think of parentheses as two cupped hands that keep one part of a sentence separated. It is so separate that the parentheses could pick it up and take it out without changing the meaning of the rest of the sentence.

The people of the town were very surprised to see the dragon (who was wearing a pin-striped suit) walking down the street with a huge front paw around the mayor's shoulders. They wondered why the dragon wasn't still in jail.

Writers use parentheses when they want to add something extra to a sentence. You can even put a whole sentence in parentheses; be sure to punctuate that sentence properly within the parentheses.

The mayor had a big smile on his face, and the dragon was cheerfully blowing smoke rings. (The dragon had once won a smoke-ring contest.) Behind them came the judge, carrying a proclamation and adjusting his spectacles.

Sometimes parentheses interrupt punctuation, and in that case the orphaned punctuation mark always comes after the second parenthesis.

What could have happened (the people wondered); what brought about this marvel?

[Brackets]

[ ]

These are called *brackets*. Brackets are used to enclose words inside a quotation. They indicate that the words inside are the writer's own words, not the words of the person who is being quoted. Most often brackets are used when you have quoted only a part of what someone said and, because you have left out some earlier words, the meaning of the sentence may not be clear without some explanation.

"I told him [the dragon] that if he wanted to get out of jail he would have to come up with a better solution, and he did," the judge told reporters.

Brackets are also used when you have parentheses within parentheses — a sorry state of affairs, but sometimes necessary.

The dragon smiled sweetly at all the photographers. (The last time there had been so much picture taking in town [July 4, 1876] was the Miss Crabapple contest.)

Dash ▬

This may look like a sleeping letter *I*, but it is actually a *dash*. Dashes are used when you need to explain something within a sentence and you want to halt the flow only briefly:

**"My solution will require many workers —
construction workers, engineers, bricklayers
— to succeed," the dragon told the crowd.**

You also use dashes when you want to make an abrupt change in the middle of a sentence:

**"I am very large and weigh about — but you
already know all that," the dragon said.**

Many writers tend to use dashes too often. Usually a comma would be better:

**The dragon — who had been thinking of this
solution for some time — was proud to tell
the town about it.**

**The dragon, who had been thinking of this
solution for some time, was proud to tell the
town about it.** *(better)*

Hyphen

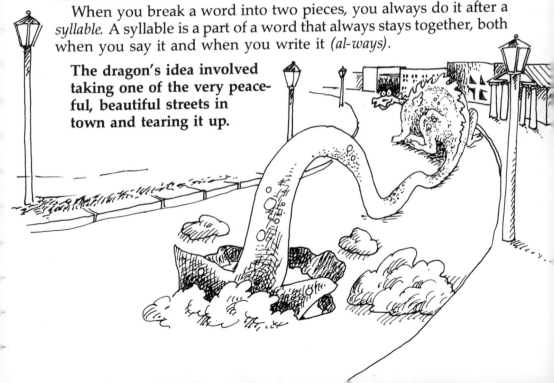

This is a *hyphen*. Think of a hyphen as glue. Hyphens are used to connect one part of a word to another or to connect several words.

Broken Words

You may have noticed in books that a bit of a word is sometimes put at the end of a line with a hyphen afterward. The word is then continued on the next line. This is called *hyphenating* words; it is done to keep all of the lines even on the right side of the page. It makes the words easier to read.

When you break a word into two pieces, you always do it after a *syllable*. A syllable is a part of a word that always stays together, both when you say it and when you write it *(al-ways)*.

The dragon's idea involved taking one of the very peace-ful, beautiful streets in town and tearing it up.

Never break a one-syllable word or a short two-syllable word. Don't separate the first letter from the rest of the word.

Everyone wondered what the dragon meant by tearing up a street. He explained that once the pavement was gone he could glide along it without sinking into it. Also, there would be a rule that no cars were al-lowed on the street.

Everyone wondered what the dragon m-eant by tearing up a street. He explained that once the pavement was gone he could glide along it without sinking into it. Also, the-re would be a rule that no cars were allowed on the street. *(wrong)*

It isn't always easy to know how a word should be hyphenated. If you don't know where to break a word, check the dictionary.

Compound Words

Compound words are words made by pushing two words together. You can write them as two words *(freight train)* or as one word *(volleyball)* or with a hyphen *(teen-ager)*.Some compound words that were once written with a hyphen are now usually written as one word. Check the dictionary to see how the compound word should be written correctly.

Here are some common uses of hyphens and compound words.

- A hyphen is used between *ex* and a noun.
  ex-knight; ex-princess; ex-criminal
- A hyphen is used to write out numbers over twenty.
  twenty-one; thirty-two; one hundred thirty-five
- Many compound words beginning with the word *self* are hyphenated.
  self-defense; self-control; self-discovery
- A hyphen is used with *un* and *anti* and *pro* and *pre* before a proper noun.
  un-American; anti-Democrat; pro-King Arthur; pre-Christian

Compound Modifiers

A compound modifier is a collection of words that come *before* a noun and describe it. When you use compound modifiers you place a hyphen between the modifiers.

bug-eyed monster; horrible-looking fiend; high-pitched scream

If the modifiers come *after* the noun, you don't need hyphens:

The fiend was horrible looking.

Apostrophe **'**

That is the *apostrophe,* which, like the vice-president, sits in for something else when it's not there.

Apostrophes are used in *contractions.* A contraction is a word made up of two words pushed together and shortened, or *contracted.* An apostrophe is placed where a missing letter or letters should be.

should not becomes *shouldn't*
do not becomes *don't*
would not becomes *wouldn't*
cannot becomes *can't*
will not becomes *won't*

The townspeople could not believe what a terrific idea the dragon had.

The townspeople couldn't believe what a terrific idea the dragon had.

Other contractions are formed by combining a pronoun *(I, we, you)* with a verb.

I will becomes *I'll*
you are becomes *you're*
we are becomes *we're*
we will becomes *we'll*

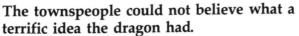

Apostrophes are also used when one or more letters or numbers have been left out of a word or numeral.

them becomes *'em*
continued becomes *cont'd*
the Spirit of 1776 becomes *the Spirit of '76*

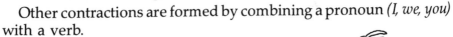

**"Let's go," cried the townspeople. "Let's tear
up that street!"**

Apostrophes are used to show that someone or something owns
something. This is called the *possessive* case. Punctuating possessives
can be very confusing. Writers often start throwing around s's and
apostrophes as if they were throwing rice at a wedding.

To nouns that don't end in s you add an apostrophe and an s to
make them possessive.

dragon's scales (the scales of one dragon)
judge's decisions (the decisions of a judge)

To plural nouns that end in s you add only the apostrophe.

dragons' scales (the scales of two or more dragons)
judges' decisions (the decisions of more than one judge)

Proper names (the name of a specific person or place) can be
troublesome. If the proper name doesn't end in s, add an apostrophe
and then an s to make it possessive.

Mr. Dragon's suit

When a name ends in s *(Charles)* there is a tendency to make the
possessive incorrectly by splitting the s off the name *(Charle's)*. When
you want to make a name ending with s possessive, add an
apostrophe *after* the first s and then add another s. Remember that
you don't want to change the spelling of the person's name.

Charles's bicycle (one bicycle belonging to someone named Charles)

A more confusing situation is a name already ending in s that you
want to make plural *and* possessive. You have to do two things to the

name: add *es* to make it plural and then add the apostrophe.

Charleses' bicycles (bicycles belonging to more than one person named Charles)

Try to slow down when you are faced with plural possessives and think carefully about what you want to say. If you go about it step by step, you will choose the right form.

Apostrophes are often misused, and it's good to watch for these common mistakes:

its and it's. Its is the possessive form *(its scales, its paw); it's* is the contraction meaning "it is" *(It is such a nice day. It's such a nice day).*

your and you're. Your is the possessive *(your fiery breath, your handsome smile); you're* is a contraction meaning "you are" *(You are a dragon with a handsome smile and fiery breath. You're a dragon with a handsome smile and fiery breath).*

their and they're. Their is the possessive *(their town, their hard work); they're* is the contraction meaning "they are" *(They are going to finish the construction soon. They're going to finish the construction soon).*

Apostrophes are also used, by the way, to form the plural of small letters.

s's; t's; w's

There are two *n's* in dungeon.

Capital letters are so much bigger than an *s* that they don't need an apostrophe.

Dragons always learn the three Bs: Breathing, Bashing, and Badminton.

/

This is the leaning tower of punctuation marks. It's called a *slash* or *bar* or *virgule.*

A bar is used when you are quoting poetry or speeches from a play and you can't or don't want to write out each line separately.

And thus the dragon's story is coming to a close./He gave free rides to all of those/Who climbed aboard his scales./They rode along the avenue/Once on top they liked the view./And the dragon liked the scratch/Of little feet along his back./The dragon had his freedom./They, in all manner dressed,/ Enjoyed the dragon's special gift – can't you guess?/A new public line of transport – /The DDD Dragon Express.

You would also use a bar when you want to indicate (or show) that either or both of two words can be used within a sentence. In a sense the bar replaces the word *or.*

The dragon said he would be happy to buy the mayor a new ten-speed bicycle and/or a pair of sneakers.

Whenever a student rode on the DDD Dragon Express, he/she was on time for school.

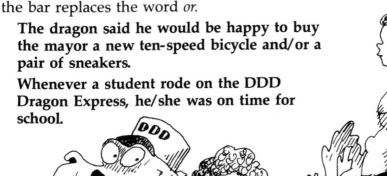

Asterisk/
Dagger

The star above is called an *asterisk*. The symbol shaped like a cross next to it is called a *dagger*.

Asterisks and daggers are used when a writer wishes to explain something to the reader, such as where certain information came from or who a character is. To avoid cluttering up the sentence, however, the writer uses an asterisk or dagger to direct the reader's attention to the bottom of the page or paragraph, where a footnote provides further explanation. You use an asterisk for the first footnote, and if you have so much to say that you need a second one, you use the dagger.

From a collection of the dragon's letters:

scp

Dear Mr. Makeadeal,*
Please send one ten-speed bicycle to the mayor. My check for $3.40 is enclosed. This should cover the cost of the bicycle as well as of a bouquet of flowers to congratulate the mayor on his upcoming celebration.†

Very truly yours,
Sir Cupcake Dragon

*Rocky Makeadeal was the town's only used-car-and-bicycle dealer.
† The celebration the dragon referred to was the mayor's fortieth birthday, July 4, 1976.

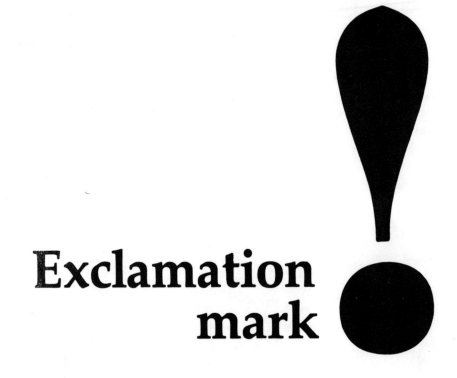

Exclamation mark

This is a period that has jumped around so much that it has turned into a permanently excited period. It is called an *exclamation mark.*

Exclamation marks express shouts, screams, threats, pleas for mercy, and other strong emotions. They are used to show shock, surprise, and commands. Unfortunately, they can't make a dull sentence exciting, and if overused, they tend to become worn out and lose their impact.

> **The mayor's fortieth birthday celebration was going very well. He laced up his new sneakers and got onto his ten-speed bicycle. The dragon got very excited and, forgetting he was in a small garden, swished his tail.**
>
> **"Watch out!" the townspeople called to the mayor, but it was too late.**
>
> **"Oh, no!" screamed the mayor as he caught the glimmer of dragon's scales coming toward him.**

You can also use an exclamation mark to make a sentence out of one word.

Help!